Introduction to Computers

and How to Purchase Computers and Mobile Devices

What Is a Computer?

Computers are everywhere: at work, at school, and at home. In the workplace, employees use computers to create correspondence such as e-mail messages, memos, and letters; manage calendars; calculate payroll; track inventory; and generate invoices. At school, teachers use computers to assist with classroom instruction. Students use computers to complete assignments and research. People also spend hours of leisure time using a computer. They play games, communicate with friends and relatives online and using e-mail, purchase goods online, converse in chat rooms, listen to music or radio broadcasts, watch or create videos and movies, read books and magazines, share stories, research genealogy, retouch photos, and plan vacations. At work, at school, and at home, computers are helping people do their work faster, more accurately, and in some cases, in ways that previously would not have been possible.

A **computer** is an electronic device, operating under the control of instructions stored in its own memory, that can accept data (input), process the data according to specified rules (process), produce results (output), and store the results (storage) for future use. Generally, the term is used to describe a collection of electric, electronic, and mechanical components known as hardware. Figure 1 shows some common hardware components. These components are discussed in more depth later in this chapter.

✋ Computers

For more information, visit scsite.com/ic8/weblink and then click Computers.

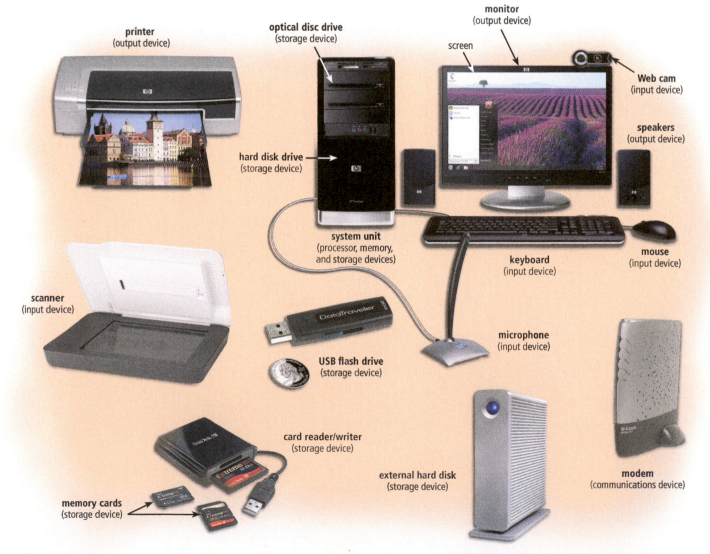

Figure 1   Common computer hardware components include the keyboard, mouse, microphone, scanner, Web cam, printer, monitor, speakers, system unit, hard disk drive, external hard disk, optical disc drive(s), USB flash drive, card reader/writer, memory cards, and modem.

Computers perform four basic operations — input, process, output, and storage. These operations comprise the **information processing cycle**. Collectively, these operations process data into information and store it for future use.

A computer derives its power from its capability to perform the information processing cycle with amazing speed, reliability (low failure rate), and accuracy; its capacity to store huge amounts of data and information; and its capability to communicate with other computers.

For a computer to perform operations, it must be given a detailed set of instructions that tells it exactly what to do. These instructions are called a program, or software. Before processing for a specific activity begins, the program corresponding to that activity is stored in the computer. Once the program is stored, the computer can begin to execute the program's first instruction. The computer executes one program instruction after another until the activity is complete.

All computer processing requires data. **Data** is a collection of unprocessed items, which can include text, numbers, images, audio, and video. Computers manipulate data to create information. **Information** conveys meaning and is useful to people. During the output operation, the information that has been created is put into some form, such as a printed report, or it can be stored on the computer for future use. As shown in Figure 2, a computer processes several data items to produce a cash register receipt.

People who use the computer directly or use the information it provides are called **computer users**, **end users**, or sometimes, just **users**. Users and computer manufacturers can reduce the environmental impact of computers through green computing. **Green computing** involves reducing the electricity consumed and environmental waste generated when using a computer.

Programs

For more information, visit scsite.com/ic8/weblink and then click Computer Programs.

Information

For more information, visit scsite.com/ic8/weblink and then click Information.

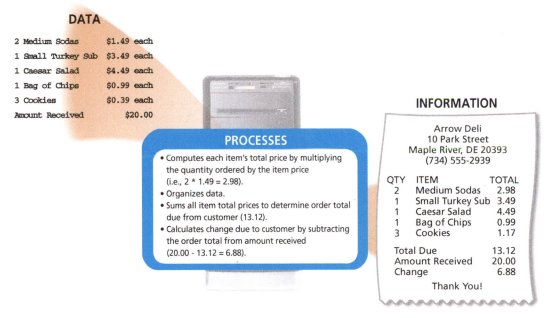

Figure 2 A computer processes data into information. In this simplified example, the item ordered, item price, quantity ordered, and amount received all represent data. The computer processes the data to produce the cash register receipt (information).

The Components of a Computer

The six primary components of a computer are input devices, the processor (control unit and arithmetic/logic unit), memory, output devices, storage devices, and communications devices. The processor, memory, and storage devices are housed in a box-like case called the system unit (shown in Figure 1). A **peripheral** is a device that connects to the system unit and is controlled by the processor in the computer. Peripherals can include input devices and output devices, as well as some storage devices and communications devices.

Figure 3 shows how the components of a computer interact to carry out a task. The following sections describe the types of personal computers and mobile devices, as well as their primary components (input devices, processor, memory, output devices, and communications devices).

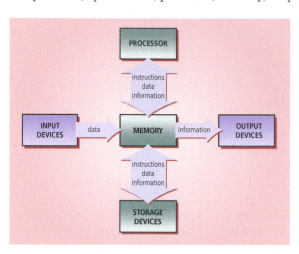

Figure 3   Most devices connected to the computer communicate with the processor to carry out a task. When a user starts a program, for example, its instructions transfer from a storage device to memory. Data needed by the program enters memory either from an input device or a storage device. The processor interprets and executes instructions in memory and also performs calculations on the data in memory. Resulting information is stored in memory, from which it can be sent to an output device or a storage device for future access, as needed.

Personal Computers and Mobile Devices

A **personal computer** is a computer that can perform all of its input, processing, output, and storage activities by itself. A personal computer contains a processor, memory, and one or more input, output, and storage devices. Personal computers also often contain a communications device. A **mobile computer** is a personal computer you can carry from place to place. Similarly, a **mobile device** is a computing device small enough to hold in your hand. The most popular type of mobile computer is the notebook computer.

Desktop Computers

A **desktop computer** is designed so that the system unit, input devices, output devices, and any other devices fit entirely on or under a desk or table (Figure 4). In some models, the monitor sits on top of the system unit, which is placed on the desk. The more popular style of system unit is the tall and narrow tower, which can sit on the floor vertically.

Figure 4   A desktop computer.

Notebook Computers

A **notebook computer**, also called a **laptop computer**, is a portable, personal computer often designed to fit on your lap (Figure 5). These computers are thin and lightweight, yet can be as powerful as the average desktop computer. A **netbook**, which is a type of notebook computer, is smaller, lighter, and often not as powerful as a traditional notebook computer. Resembling a letter-sized slate, the **Tablet PC** is a special type of notebook computer that allows you to write or draw on the screen using a digital pen.

Mobile Devices

Mobile devices, which are small enough to carry in a pocket, usually store programs and data permanently on memory inside the system unit or on small storage media such as memory cards. You often can connect a mobile device to a personal computer to exchange information. Three popular types of mobile devices are smart phones, portable media players, and digital cameras.

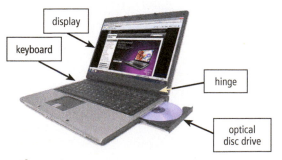

Figure 5   A traditional notebook computer.

A **smart phone** is a phone that can connect to the Internet and usually also provides personal information management functions such as a calendar, an appointment book, an address book, a calculator, and a notepad (Figure 6). A **portable media player** is a mobile device on which you can store, organize, and play digital media (shown in Figure 1 on page COM 2). For example, you can listen to music; watch videos, movies, and television shows; and view photos on the device's screen. A **digital camera** is a device that allows users to take pictures and store the photographed images digitally, instead of on traditional film (shown in Figure 1). Digital cameras typically allow users to review, and sometimes modify, images while they are in the camera.

Figure 6   A smart phone is a popular mobile device.

Input Devices

An **input device** is any hardware component that allows you to enter data and instructions into a computer. Depending on your particular program and requirements, the input device you use may vary. Five widely used input devices are the keyboard, mouse, microphone, scanner, and Web cam (shown in Figure 1). The two primary input devices used are the keyboard and the mouse.

Keyboard

A **keyboard** is an input device that contains keys users press to enter data and instructions into the computer. All desktop computer keyboards have a typing area that includes the letters of the alphabet, numbers, punctuation marks, and other basic keys. Many desktop computer keyboards also have a numeric keypad on the right side of the keyboard. Most of today's desktop computer keyboards are enhanced keyboards. An enhanced keyboard has 12 or more function keys along the top and a set of arrow and additional keys between the typing area and the numeric keypad (Figure 7). Function keys are special keys programmed to issue instructions to a computer.

👆 **Input Devices**

For more information, visit scsite.com/ic8/weblink and then click Input Devices.

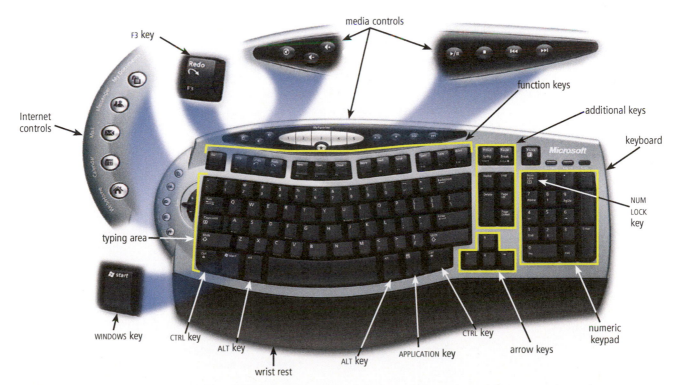

Figure 7   On a desktop computer keyboard, you type using keys in the typing area and on the numeric keypad.

A variety of options are available for typing on a smart phone (Figure 8). Many can display an on-screen keyboard, where you press the on-screen keys using your finger or a stylus. A **stylus** is a small metal or plastic device that looks like a tiny ink pen but uses pressure instead of ink. Some smart phones have one key for each letter of the alphabet, often called a mini-keyboard. Other phones have keypads that contain fewer keys than there are letters in the alphabet. For these phones, each key on the keypad represents multiple characters, which are identified on the key.

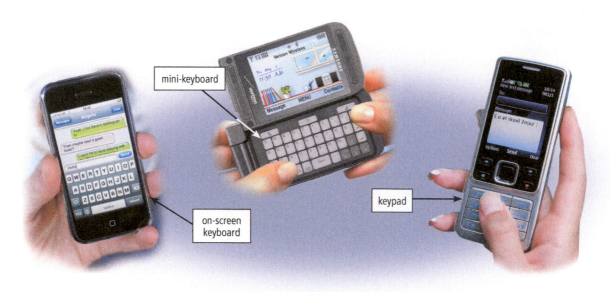

Figure 8   Users have a variety of options for typing on a phone.

Mouse and Other Pointing Devices

A **mouse** is a pointing device that fits comfortably under the palm of your hand (Figure 9). With a mouse, users control the movement of the **pointer**, which is a small symbol on the screen whose location and shape change as a user moves a pointing device. As you move a mouse, for example, the pointer on the screen also moves. Generally, you use the mouse to move the pointer on the screen to an object such as a button, a menu, an icon, a link, or text. Then, you press a mouse button to perform a certain action associated with that object. The bottom of a mouse is flat and contains a mechanism (ball, optical sensor, or laser sensor) that detects movement of the mouse.

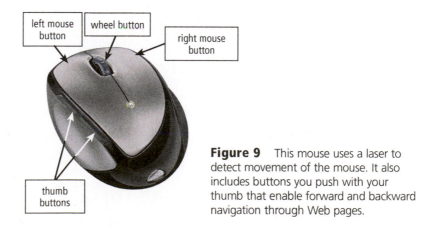

Figure 9   This mouse uses a laser to detect movement of the mouse. It also includes buttons you push with your thumb that enable forward and backward navigation through Web pages.

Most notebook computers have a **touchpad**, a small, flat, rectangular pointing device near the keyboard that allows you to move the pointer by sliding a fingertip on the surface of the pad (Figure 10).

Figure 10   Most notebook computers have a touchpad that allows a user to control the movement of the pointer.

Other Input for Mobile Devices   Most mobile devices, such as smart phones and PDAs, and some notebook computers, such as Tablet PCs, use a variety of alternatives for entering data and instructions (Figure 11). One of the more popular input devices for mobile devices is the stylus. Some have touch screens, enabling you to touch the screen to perform tasks.

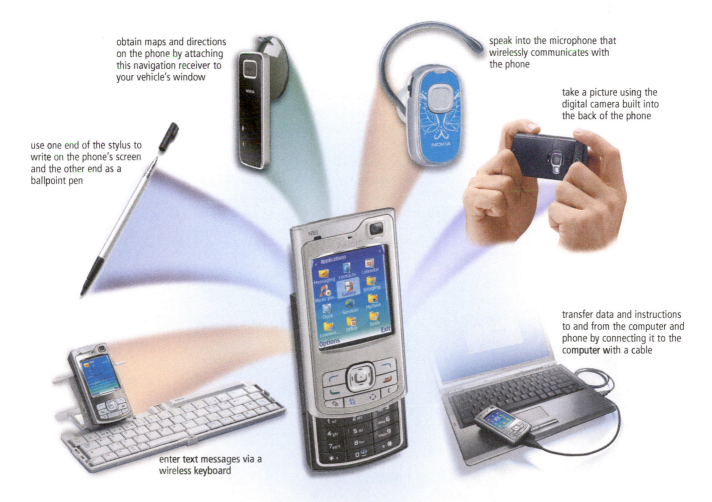

obtain maps and directions on the phone by attaching this navigation receiver to your vehicle's window

speak into the microphone that wirelessly communicates with the phone

take a picture using the digital camera built into the back of the phone

use one end of the stylus to write on the phone's screen and the other end as a ballpoint pen

transfer data and instructions to and from the computer and phone by connecting it to the computer with a cable

enter text messages via a wireless keyboard

Figure 11   Besides a touch screen and basic stylus, users have a variety of other options for entering data and instructions into a smart phone.

System Unit

The **system unit** is a case that contains electronic components of the computer used to process data (Figure 12). System units are available in a variety of shapes and sizes. The case of the system unit, also called the chassis, is made of metal or plastic and protects the internal components from damage. The **motherboard**, sometimes called a system board, is the main circuit board of the system unit. Many electronic components attach to the motherboard; others are built into it. The sound card and video card shown in Figure 12 are examples of adapter cards, which are circuit boards that provide connections and functions not built into the motherboard or expand on the capability of features integrated into the motherboard.

Processor

The **processor** (bottom of Figure 12), also called the **central processing unit** (**CPU**), interprets and carries out the basic instructions that operate a computer. Processors contain a control unit and an arithmetic/logic unit. The **control unit** directs and coordinates most of the operations in the computer. The **arithmetic/logic unit** (**ALU**) performs arithmetic, comparison, and other operations.

On a personal computer, all functions of the processor usually are on a single chip. A computer chip is a small piece of semiconducting material that contains many microscopic pathways capable of carrying electrical current. Today's processors can perform some operations in less than the time it takes to blink your eye.

Processor

For more information, visit scsite.com/ic8/weblink and then click Processor.

Memory

Memory consists of electronic components that store instructions waiting to be executed and data needed by those instructions. Most memory keeps data and instructions temporarily, which means its contents are erased when the computer is shut off. When discussing computer memory, users typically are referring to RAM. Also called main memory, **RAM** (random access memory) consists of memory chips that can be read from and written to by the processor and other devices. These chips are placed on a memory module (lower left of Figure 12) that fits in a slot on the motherboard in the system unit.

The amount of memory in computers is measured in kilobytes, megabytes, gigabytes, or terabytes. A **byte** usually stores one character, such as the letter A. One **kilobyte** (**KB or K**) equals exactly 1,024 bytes, and one **megabyte** (**MB**) equals approximately one million bytes. One **gigabyte** (**GB**) equals approximately one billion bytes, and one **terabyte** (**TB**) equals approximately

Memory

For more information, visit scsite.com/ic8/weblink and then click Memory.

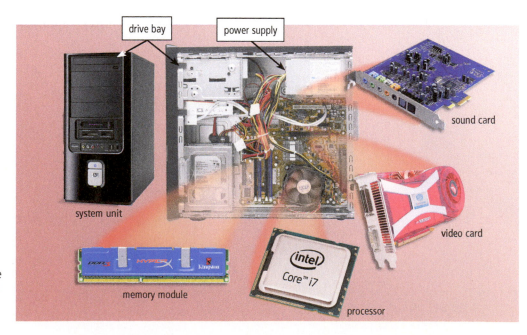

drive bay

power supply

sound card

system unit

video card

memory module

processor

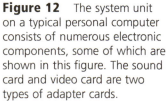
Figure 12 The system unit on a typical personal computer consists of numerous electronic components, some of which are shown in this figure. The sound card and video card are two types of adapter cards.

one trillion bytes. A computer with 4 GB of RAM, therefore, can store approximately four billion characters. For reference, one megabyte can hold approximately 500 letter-size pages of text information, and one gigabyte can hold approximately 500,000 letter-size pages of text information.

Output Devices

Output devices are hardware components that convey information to one or more people. Commonly used output devices include display devices; printers; speakers, headphones, and earbuds; data projectors; and interactive whiteboards. When a computer is used for processing tasks such as creating documents, the two output devices widely used are the printer and a display device.

🖑 **Output Devices**

For more information, visit scsite.com/ic8/weblink and then click Output Devices.

Printers

A **printer** is an output device that produces text and graphics on a physical medium such as paper. Ink-jet printers and laser printers often are used with personal computers.

Ink-jet printers produce text and graphics in both black and white and color on a variety of paper types and sizes (Figure 13). Some ink-jet printers, called **photo printers**, produce photo-lab-quality pictures and are ideal for home or small-business use. The speed of an ink-jet printer is measured by the number of pages per minute (ppm) it can print. Most ink-jet printers print from 12 to 36 pages per minute. Graphics and colors print at the slower rate.

A **laser printer** is a high-speed, high-quality printer that operates in a manner similar to a copy machine (Figure 14). Laser printers typically use individual sheets of paper stored in one or more removable trays that slide in the printer case. It creates images using a laser beam and powdered ink, called toner, on a special drum inside the printer, forming the images to be printed. Laser printers can cost from a couple hundred dollars to a few thousand dollars for the home and small office user, to several hundred thousand dollars for large business users. Generally, the more expensive the laser printer, the more pages it can print per minute.

A **multifunction peripheral**, also called an **all-in-one device**, is a single device that looks like a printer or copy machine but provides the functionality of a printer, scanner, copy machine, and perhaps a fax machine. Some use color ink-jet printer technology, while others include a black-and-white or color laser printer.

Figure 13   Ink-jet printers are a popular type of color printer used in the home.

Figure 14   A color laser printer.

Display Devices

A **display device** is an output device that visually conveys text, graphics, and video information. A **monitor** is a display device that is packaged as a separate peripheral. A widely used monitor is an LCD monitor. The **LCD monitor** shown in Figure 15 uses a liquid crystal display to produce images on the screen. The surface of the screen of an LCD monitor is composed of individual picture elements called **pixels**. **Resolution** is the number of horizontal and vertical pixels in a display device. For example, a screen set to a resolution of 1440 × 900 pixels displays up to 1440 pixels per horizontal row and 900 pixels per vertical row, for a total of 1,296,000 pixels to create a screen image. A higher resolution provides a smoother, sharper, clearer image.

Mobile computers such as notebook computers, including netbooks and Tablet PCs, and mobile devices such as smart phones, portable media players, PDAs, handheld game consoles, and digital cameras, have built-in LCD screens (Figure 16).

speakers

Figure 15 The LCD monitor is widely used with desktop computers.

notebook computer

PDA

smart phone

handheld game console

portable media player

digital camera

Figure 16 Notebook computers, PDAs, smart phones, handheld game consoles, portable media players, and digital cameras have color LCD screens.

Storage Devices

A **storage device** is the computer hardware that records and/or retrieves items to and from storage media. A **storage medium** (media is the plural) is the physical material on which a computer keeps data, instructions, and information. Three common types of storage media are hard disks, flash memory, and optical discs.

Hard Disks

A **hard disk** is a storage device that contains one or more inflexible, circular platters that use magnetic particles to store data, instructions, and information. The system unit on most personal computers contains at least one hard disk, sometimes called an internal hard disk because it is not portable. Users store documents, spreadsheets, presentations, databases, e-mail messages, Web pages, digital photos, music, videos, and software on hard disks.

Hard disks store data and instructions in tracks and sectors on a platter (Figure 17). A **track** is a narrow recording band that forms a full circle on the surface of the disk. The disk's storage locations consist of pie-shaped sections, which break the tracks into small arcs called **sectors**. On a hard disk, a sector typically stores up to 512 bytes of data. Storage capacities of internal hard disks for personal computers range from 160 GB to more than 2 TB.

On desktop computers, platters most often have a size of approximately 3.5 inches in diameter. On notebook computers and mobile devices, the diameter is 2.5 inches or less. A typical hard disk has multiple platters stacked on top of one another. Each platter has two read/write heads, one for each side. The hard disk has arms that move the read/write heads to the proper location on the platter (Figure 18). The hard disk platters spin at a high rate of speed, typically 5,400 to 15,000 revolutions per minute. On today's computers, the platters typically stop spinning or slow down after a specified time to save power.

When reading or writing, the read/write heads on a hard disk do not actually touch the surface of the disk. The distance between the read/write heads and the platters is about two millionths of one inch. This close clearance means that dirt, hair, dust, smoke, or other particles could cause the hard disk to have a **head crash**, when a read/write head touches a platter, usually resulting in loss of data or sometimes the entire disk. Although current hard disks are sealed tightly to keep out contaminants, head crashes do occur occasionally. Thus, it is crucial that you back up your hard disk regularly. A **backup** is a duplicate of a file, program, or disk placed on a separate storage medium that you can use in case the original is lost, damaged, or destroyed.

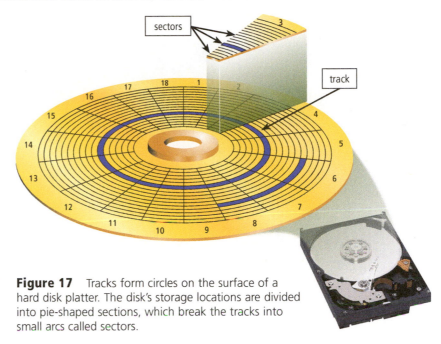

Figure 17 Tracks form circles on the surface of a hard disk platter. The disk's storage locations are divided into pie-shaped sections, which break the tracks into small arcs called sectors.

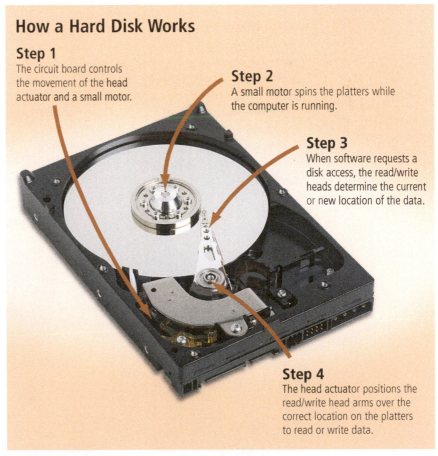

How a Hard Disk Works

Step 1
The circuit board controls the movement of the head actuator and a small motor.

Step 2
A small motor spins the platters while the computer is running.

Step 3
When software requests a disk access, the read/write heads determine the current or new location of the data.

Step 4
The head actuator positions the read/write head arms over the correct location on the platters to read or write data.

Figure 18 This figure shows how a hard disk works.

Portable Hard Disks   Some hard disks are portable. An **external hard disk** (Figure 19) is a separate freestanding hard disk that connects with a cable to a port on the system unit or communicates wirelessly. A **removable hard disk** (Figure 20) is a hard disk that you insert and remove from a drive. Both internal and external hard disks are available in miniature sizes to allow users to transport their data easily.

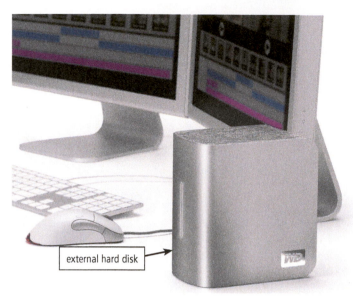

Figure 19   An external hard disk.

Figure 20   A removable hard disk.

Flash Memory Storage

Flash memory is a type of memory that can be erased electronically and rewritten. Flash memory chips are a type of **solid state media**, which means they consist entirely of electronic components and contain no moving parts. Types of flash memory storage include solid state drives, memory cards, USB flash drives, and ExpressCard modules.

Flash Memory Storage

For more information, visit scsite.com/ic8/weblink and then click Flash Memory Storage.

A **solid state drive** (**SSD**) is a storage device that typically uses flash memory to store data, instructions, and information (Figure 21). With available sizes of 3.5 inches, 2.5 inches, and 1.8 inches, SSDs are used in all types of computers, including desktop computers, mobile computers, and mobile devices such as portable media players and digital video cameras. Storage capacities of current SSDs range from 16 GB to 256 GB and more.

Figure 21   As the price of SSDs drops, experts estimate that increasingly more users will purchase computers and devices that use this media.

A **memory card** is a removable flash memory device, usually no bigger than 1.5 inches in height or width, that you insert and remove from a slot in a computer, mobile device, or card reader/writer (Figure 22). Memory cards enable mobile users easily to transport digital photos, music, or files to and from mobile devices and computers or other devices.

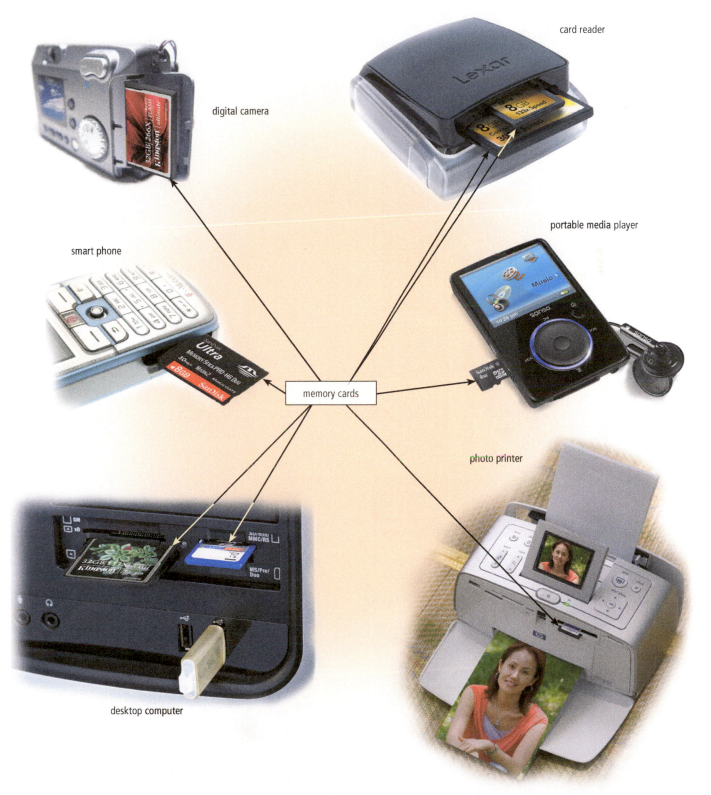

Figure 22   Many types of computers and devices have slots for memory cards.

Common types of memory cards include CompactFlash (CF), Secure Digital (SD), Secure Digital High Capacity (SDHC), microSD, microSDHC, xD Picture Card, Memory Stick PRO Duo, and Memory Stick Micro (M2) (Figure 23).

Various Memory Cards

Media Type		Storage Capacity	Use
CompactFlash (CF)		512 MB to 100 GB	Digital cameras, smart phones, PDAs, photo printers, portable media players, notebook computers, desktop computers
Secure Digital (SD)		512 MB to 8 GB	Digital cameras, digital video cameras, smart phones, PDAs, photo printers, portable media players
SDHC		4 to 32 GB	Digital cameras
microSD		1 to 2 GB	Smart phones, portable media players, handheld game consoles, handheld navigation devices
microSDHC		4 to 16 GB	Smart phones, portable media players, handheld game consoles, handheld navigation devices
xD Picture Card	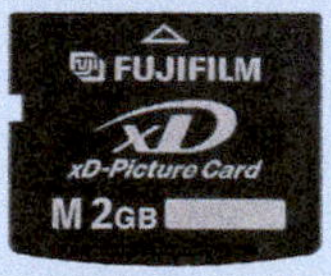	256 MB to 2 GB	Digital cameras, photo printers
Memory Stick PRO Duo		1 to 16 GB	Digital cameras, smart phones, handheld game consoles
Memory Stick Micro (M2)	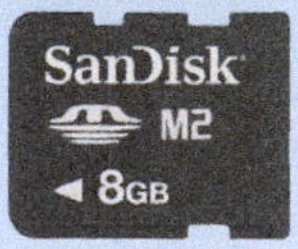	1 to 16 GB	Smart phones

Figure 23   A variety of memory cards.

A **USB flash drive**, sometimes called a thumb drive, is a flash memory storage device that plugs into a USB port on a computer or mobile device (Figure 24). USB flash drives are convenient for mobile users because they are small and light-weight enough to be transported on a keychain or in a pocket. Current USB flash drives have storage capacities ranging from 512 MB to 64 GB.

An **ExpressCard module** is a removable device, about 75 mm long and 34 mm wide or L-shaped with a width of 54 mm, that fits in an ExpressCard slot (Figure 25). ExpressCard modules can be used to add memory, storage, communications, multimedia, and security capabilities to a computer. ExpressCard modules commonly are used in notebook computers.

Figure 24   A close-up of the flash memory and circuitry inside a USB flash drive.

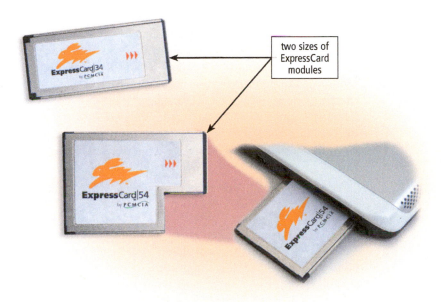

two sizes of ExpressCard modules

Figure 25   ExpressCard modules are available in two sizes.

Optical Discs

An **optical disc** is a flat, round, portable metal disc with a plastic coating. CDs, DVDs, and Blu-ray Discs are three types of optical discs. A CD can hold from 650 million to 1 billion characters. Some DVDs can store two full-length movies or 17 billion characters. Blu-ray Discs can store about 46 hours of standard video, or 100 billion characters. Optical discs used in personal computers are 4.75 inches in diameter and less than one-twentieth of an inch thick. Nearly every personal computer today has some type of optical disc drive installed in a drive bay. On some, you push a button to slide out a tray, insert the disc, and then push the same button to close the tray; others are slot loaded, which means you insert the disc in a narrow opening on the drive (Figure 26).

Figure 26   A slot-loaded optical disc drive.

Optical Disc Formats

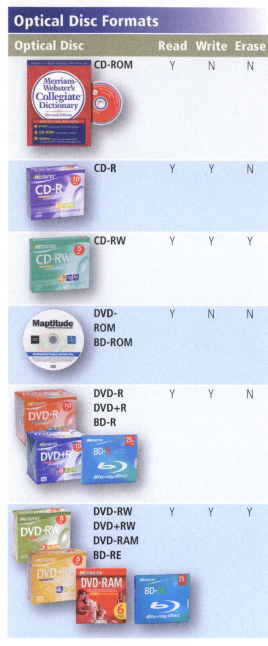

Optical Disc	Read	Write	Erase
CD-ROM	Y	N	N
CD-R	Y	Y	N
CD-RW	Y	Y	Y
DVD-ROM BD-ROM	Y	N	N
DVD-R DVD+R BD-R	Y	Y	N
DVD-RW DVD+RW DVD-RAM BD-RE	Y	Y	Y

Figure 27 Manufacturers sell CD-ROM, DVD-ROM, and BD-ROM media prerecorded (written) with audio, video, and software. Users cannot change the contents of these discs. Users, however, can purchase the other formats of optical discs as blank media and record (write) their own data, instructions, and information on these discs.

👆 **CDs**

For more information, visit scsite.com/ic8/weblink and then click CDs.

Many different formats of optical discs exist today. Figure 27 identifies a variety of optical disc formats and specifies whether a user can read from the disc, write on the disc, and/or erase the disc.

A **CD-ROM,** or compact disc read-only memory, is a type of optical disc that users can read but not write (record) or erase — hence, the name read-only. Manufacturers write the contents of standard CD-ROMs. A standard CD-ROM is called a single-session disc because manufacturers write all items on the disc at one time. Software manufacturers often distribute programs using CD-ROMs.

A typical CD-ROM holds from 650 MB to 1 GB of data, instructions, and information. To read a CD-ROM, insert the disc in a CD-ROM drive or a CD-ROM player. Because audio CDs and CD-ROMs use the same laser technology, you may be able to use a CD-ROM drive to listen to an audio CD while using the computer.

A **CD-R** (compact disc-recordable) is a multisession optical disc on which users can write, but not erase, their own items such as text, graphics, and audio. Multisession means you can write on part of the disc at one time and another part at a later time. Each part of a CD-R can be written on only one time, and the disc's contents cannot be erased.

A **CD-RW** (compact disc-rewritable) is an erasable multisession disc you can write on multiple times. To write on a CD-RW disc, you must have optical disc burning software and a CD-RW drive. Burning is the process of writing on an optical disc. A popular use of CD-RW and CD-R discs is to create audio CDs. For example, users can record their own music and save it on a CD, purchase and download songs from the Web to their computer and then burn the songs on a CD, or rearrange tracks on a purchased music CD. The process of copying audio and/or video data from a purchased disc and saving it on a storage medium is called ripping.

Although CDs have large storage capacities, even a CD cannot hold many of today's complex programs. Thus, some software companies have moved from CDs to the larger DVDs — a technology that can be used to store large amounts of text and even videos (Figure 28).

A **DVD-ROM** (digital versatile disk-read-only memory or digital video disc-read-only memory) is a high-capacity optical disc on which users can read but not write or erase. Manufacturers write the contents of DVD-ROMs and distribute them to consumers. DVD-ROMs store movies, music, huge databases, and complex software. To read a DVD-ROM, you need a **DVD-ROM drive** or DVD player. Most DVD-ROM drives also can read audio CDs, CD-ROMs, CD-Rs, and CD-RWs.

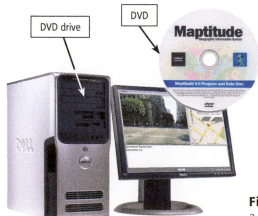

Figure 28 A DVD-ROM is a high-capacity optical disc.

A newer, more expensive DVD format is Blu-ray, which is a higher capacity and better quality than standard DVDs, especially for high-definition audio and video. A **Blu-ray Disc** (BD) has storage capacities of 100 GB, with expectations of exceeding 200 GB in the future.

Many types of recordable and rewritable DVD formats are available. DVD-R, DVD+R, and BD-R allow users to write on the disc once and read (play) it many times. **DVD-RW, DVD+RW, and DVD+RAM** are three competing rewritable DVD formats. Similarly, **BD-RE** is a high-capacity rewritable Blu-ray format. To write on these discs, you must have a compatible drive or recorder.

 DVDs

For more information, visit scsite.com/ic8/weblink and then click DVDs.

Cloud Storage

Cloud storage is an Internet service that provides hard disk storage to computer users (Figure 29). Fee arrangements vary. For example, one cloud storage service provides 25 GB of storage free to registered users; another charges $5 per month for 150 GB of storage. For organizations, cloud storage services typically charge for storage on a per gigabyte basis, such as 15 cents per gigabyte.

Types of services offered by cloud storage providers vary. Figure 30 identifies a variety of cloud storage providers.

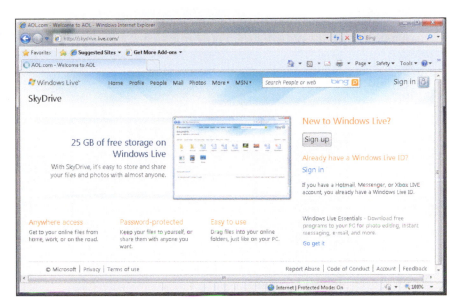

Figure 29   An example of one Web site advertising its storage service.

Cloud Storage Providers	
Web Site Names	**Type of Storage Provided**
Box.net, IDrive, Windows Live SkyDrive	Backup or additional storage for any type of file
Flickr, Picasa	Digital photos
YouTube	Digital videos
Facebook, MySpace	Digital photos, digital videos, messages, and personal information
Google Docs	Documents, spreadsheets, presentations
Gmail, Windows Live Hotmail, Yahoo! Mail	E-mail messages
Amazon EC2, Amazon S3, Nirvanix	Enterprise-level storage

Figure 30   Some of the more widely used cloud storage providers.

Communications Devices

A **communications device** is a hardware component that enables a computer to send (transmit) and receive data, instructions, and information to and from one or more computers or mobile devices. A widely used communications device is a modem (Figure 1 on page COM 2).

Communications occur over **transmission media** such as cables, telephone lines, cellular radio networks, and satellites. Some transmission media, such as satellites and cellular radio networks, are **wireless**, which means they have no physical lines or wires. People around the world use computers and communications devices to communicate with each other using one or more transmission media.

Computer Software

Software, also called a **program,** consists of a series of related instructions, organized for a common purpose, that tells the computer what tasks to perform and how to perform them. You interact with a program through its user interface. The user interface controls how you enter data and instructions and how information is displayed on the screen. Software today often has a graphical user interface. With a **graphical user interface** (**GUI** pronounced gooey), you interact with the software using text, graphics, and visual images such as icons.

When you buy a computer, it usually has some software on its hard disk. This enables you to use the computer the first time you turn it on. Programs also can be installed after you purchase the computer. **Installing** is the process of adding software to a computer, and **uninstalling** is the process of removing programs and all associated files from the hard disk.

Much software is available at retail stores and on the Web for purchase and/or download. As an alternative, some people use a **Web application,** which is a Web site that allows users to access and interact with software from any computer or device that is connected to the Internet. Software can be divided into two categories: system software and application software (Figure 31).

Figure 31   Today's system software and application software usually have a graphical user interface.

System Software

System software consists of programs that control the operations of the computer and its devices. Two types of system software are operating systems and utility programs.

An **operating system** is a set of programs that coordinates all the activities among computer hardware devices. It provides a means for users to communicate with the computer and other software. Many of today's computers use Microsoft Windows, the latest version of which is shown in Figure 31, or Mac OS, Apple's operating system. When a user starts a computer, portions of the operating system are copied into memory from the computer's hard disk. These parts of the operating system remain in memory while the computer is on.

A **utility program** allows a user to perform maintenance-type tasks usually related to managing a computer, its devices, or its programs. For example, you can use a utility program to burn digital photos on an optical disc. Most operating systems include several utility programs for managing disk drives, printers, and other devices and media. You also can buy utility programs that allow you to perform additional computer management functions.

Application Software

Application software consists of programs designed to make users more productive and/or assist them with personal tasks. These include personal information management, note taking, project management, accounting, document management, computer-aided design, desktop publishing, paint/image editing, audio and video editing, multimedia authoring, Web page authoring, personal finance, legal, tax preparation, home design/landscaping, travel and mapping, education, reference, and entertainment (e.g., games or simulations). Software is available at stores that sell computer products and at many Web sites.

Computer users regularly use application software. Some of the more commonly used programs are word processing, presentation, spreadsheet, database, and e-mail. These programs often are sold together as a unit, called a business suite. When you purchase a collection of programs as a suite, the suite usually costs significantly less than purchasing them individually. Suites also provide ease of use because the programs in the suite normally use a similar interface and share features.

Operating Systems
For more information, visit scsite.com/ic8/weblink and then click Operating Systems.

Word Processing   **Word processing software** is used to create, edit, format, and print documents (Figure 32). A key advantage of word processing software is that users easily can make changes in documents, such as correcting spelling; changing margins; and adding, deleting, or relocating words, sentences, or entire paragraphs.

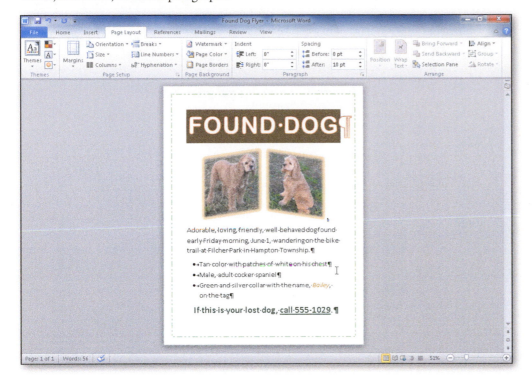

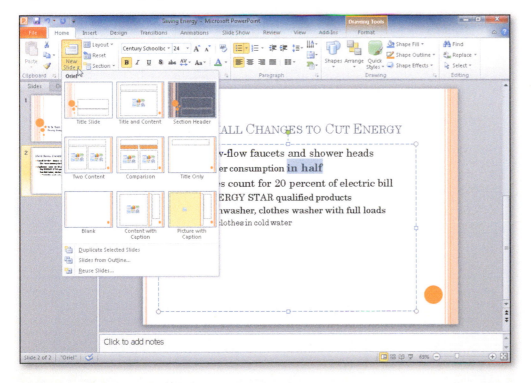

Word Processing Software

For more information, visit scsite.com/ic8/weblink and then click Word Processing Software.

Figure 32   Word processing software is used to create letters, memos, newsletters, and other documents.

Presentation   **Presentation software** is application software that allows users to create visual aids for presentations to communicate ideas, messages, and other information to a group (Figure 33). The presentations can be viewed as slides, sometimes called a slide show, that are displayed on a large monitor or on a projection screen.

Presentation Software

For more information, visit scsite.com/ic8/weblink and then click Presentation Software.

Figure 33   Presentation software allows the user to produce professional-looking presentations.

Spreadsheet **Spreadsheet software** allows users to organize data in rows and columns and perform calculations on the data (Figure 34). These rows and columns collectively are called a **worksheet**. Most spreadsheet software has basic features to help users create, edit, and format worksheets.

🖐 **Spreadsheet Software**

For more information, visit scsite.com/ic8/weblink and then click Spreadsheet Software.

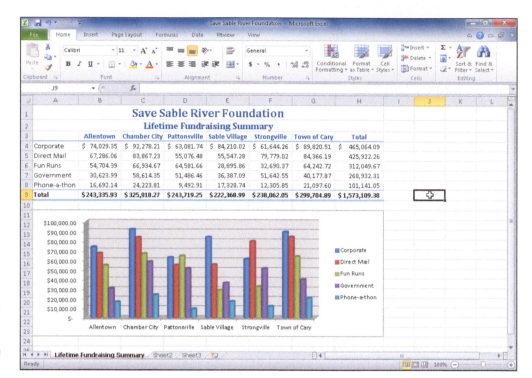

Figure 34 With spreadsheet software, you create worksheets that contain data arranged in rows and columns, and you can perform calculations on the data in the worksheets.

Database A **database** is a collection of data organized in a manner that allows access, retrieval, and use of that data. **Database software** is application software that allows users to create, access, and manage a database (Figure 35). Using database software, you can add, change, and delete data in a database; sort and retrieve data from the database; and create forms and reports using the data in the database.

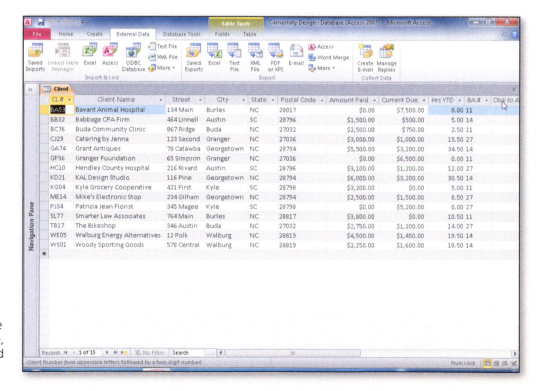

🖐 **Database Software**

For more information, visit scsite.com/ic8/weblink and then click Database Software.

Figure 35 Database software allows the user to enter, retrieve, and update data in an organized and efficient manner.

E-Mail E-mail (short for electronic mail) is the transmission of messages and files via a computer network. Today, e-mail is a primary communications method for both personal and business use. You use an **e-mail program** to create, send, receive, forward, store, print, and delete e-mail messages (Figure 36). Outlook and Windows Live Mail are two popular desktop e-mail programs. Just as you address a letter when using the postal system, you address an e-mail message with the e-mail address of your intended recipient. Likewise, when someone sends you a message, he or she must have your e-mail address.

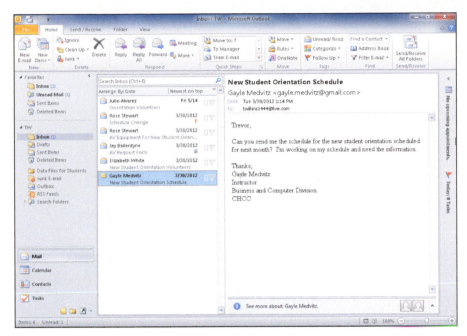

Figure 36 An e-mail program.

Networks and the Internet

A **network** is a collection of computers and devices connected together, often wirelessly, via communications devices and transmission media. When a computer connects to a network, it is **online**. Networks allow users to share resources, such as hardware, software, data, and information. Sharing resources saves time and money. For example, instead of purchasing one printer for every computer in a company, the firm can connect a single printer and all computers via a network; the network enables all of the computers to access the same printer.

Most business computers are networked. These networks can be relatively small or quite extensive. A **local area network** (**LAN**) is a network that connects computers and devices in a limited geographical area such as a home, school computer laboratory, office building, or closely positioned group of buildings. A **wireless LAN** (**WLAN**) is a LAN that uses no physical wires. Often, a WLAN communicates with a wired LAN (Figure 37).

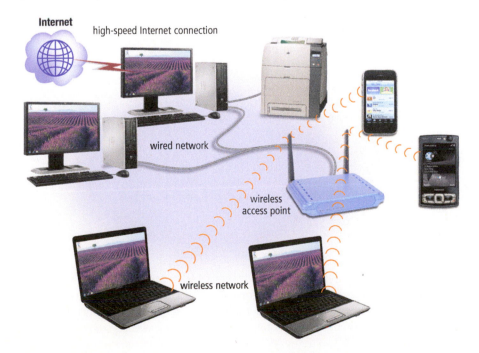

Figure 37 Computers and mobile devices on a wireless LAN often communicate via an access point with a wired LAN to access its software, printer, the Internet, and other resources.

A **wide area network** (**WAN**) is a network that covers a large geographic area (such as a city, country, or the world) using a communications channel that combines many types of media such as telephone lines, cables, and radio waves (Figure 38). The Internet is the world's largest WAN.

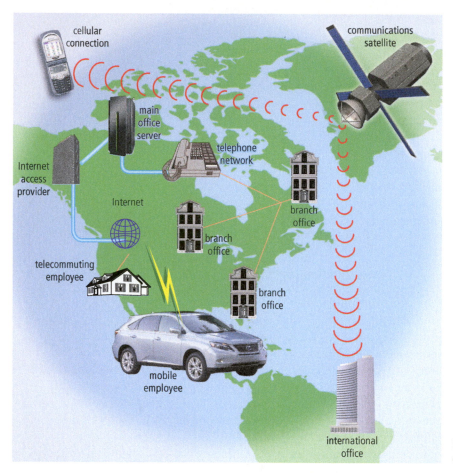

Figure 38 An example of a WAN.

The Internet

The **Internet** is a worldwide collection of networks that links millions of businesses, government agencies, educational institutions, and individuals. With an abundance of resources and data accessible via the Internet, more than one billion people around the world use the Internet for a variety of reasons, including the following (Figure 39):

- Communicating with and meeting other people
- Researching and accessing a wealth of information and news
- Shopping for goods and services
- Banking and investing
- Participating in online training
- Engaging in entertaining activities, such as planning vacations, playing online games, listening to music, watching or editing videos, and reading books and magazines
- Sharing information, photos, and videos
- Downloading music and videos
- Accessing and interacting with Web applications

An **access provider** is a business that provides individuals and organizations access to the Internet free or for a fee. Access providers are categorized as ISPs, online service providers, and wireless Internet service providers. An **ISP** (**Internet service provider**) is a regional or national access provider. A regional ISP usually provides Internet access to a specific geographic area.

Figure 39 Users access the Internet for a variety of reasons.

A national ISP is a business that provides Internet access in cities and towns nationwide. National ISPs usually offer more services and have a larger technical support staff than regional ISPs. Examples of national ISPs are AT&T and EarthLink. In addition to providing Internet access, an **online service provider** (**OSP**) also has many members-only features such as instant messaging or their own customized version of a Web browser. The two more popular OSPs are AOL (America Online) and MSN (Microsoft Network).

A **wireless Internet service provider**, sometimes called a wireless data provider, is a company that provides wireless Internet access to computers and mobile devices, such as smart phones and portable media players, with built-in wireless capability (such as Wi-Fi) or to computers using wireless modems or wireless access devices. Wireless modems usually are in the form of a USB flash drive or a card that inserts in a slot in a computer or mobile device. Examples of wireless Internet service providers include AT&T, Sprint Broadband Direct, T-Mobile, and Verizon Wireless.

The World Wide Web

One of the more popular services on the Internet is the **World Wide Web**, also called the **Web**, which contains billions of documents called Web pages. A **Web page** can contain text, graphics, animation, audio, and video, and has built-in connections, or links, to other documents, graphics, or other Web pages. Web pages are stored on computers throughout the world. A **Web site** is a collection of related Web pages. Visitors to a Web site access and view Web pages using a program called a **Web browser**. A Web page has a unique address, called a **Web address** or **URL** (**Uniform Resource Locator**).

As shown in Figure 40, a Web address consists of a protocol, a domain name, sometimes the path to a specific Web page or location in a Web page, and the Web page name. Many Web page addresses begin with **http://**, which stands for **Hypertext Transfer Protocol**, the set of rules that defines how pages transfer on the Internet. The domain name identifies the Web site, which is stored on a Web server. A **Web server** is a computer that delivers requested Web pages to your computer.

The term **Web 2.0** refers to Web sites that provide a means for users to share personal information (such as social networking Web sites), allow users to modify the Web site contents (such as some blogs), and/or have software built into the site for users to access (such as Web applications). A **social networking Web site** or **online social network** is an online community that encourages members to share their interests, ideas, stories, photos, music, and videos with other registered users. A **blog** is an informal Web site consisting of time-stamped articles in a diary or journal format. Examples of software available as Web applications include those that allow you to send and receive e-mail messages, prepare your taxes, organize digital photos, create documents, and play games.

🖑 **World Wide Web**

For more information, visit scsite.com/ic8/weblink and then click World Wide Web.

protocol	domain name		path		Web page name

http://www.nps.gov/grsm/planyourvist/wildlifeviewing.htm

Figure 40   After entering http://www.nps.gov/grsm/planyourvist/wildlifeviewing.htm as the Web address in the Address bar, this Web page at the United States National Park Service Web site is displayed.

E-commerce, short for electronic commerce, is a business transaction that occurs over an electronic network such as the Internet. Anyone with access to a computer or mobile device, an Internet connection, and a means to pay for purchased goods or services can participate in e-commerce.

Searching the Web

The Web is a worldwide resource of information. A primary reason that people use the Web is to search for specific information, including text, pictures, music, and video. The first step in successful searching is to identify the main idea or concept in the topic about which you are seeking information. Determine any synonyms, alternate spellings, or variant word forms for the topic. Then, use a search tool to locate the information.

Two types of search tools are search engines and subject directories. A **search engine** is a program that finds Web sites, Web pages, images, videos, news, maps, and other information related to a specific topic. A search engine is helpful in locating information for which you do not know an exact Web address or are not seeking a particular Web site. Search engines require that you enter a word or phrase, called **search text**, that describes the item you want to find. Figure 41 shows one way to use the Google search engine to search for the phrase, Aspen Colorado ski resorts. A **subject directory** classifies Web pages in an organized set of categories or groups, such as sports or

👆 **E-Commerce**

For more information, visit scsite.com/ic8/weblink and then click E-Commerce.

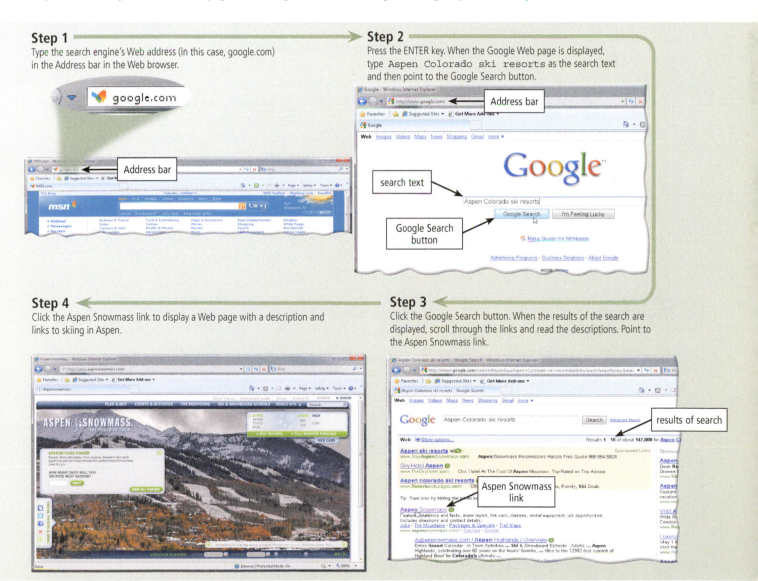

Step 1
Type the search engine's Web address (in this case, google.com) in the Address bar in the Web browser.

Step 2
Press the ENTER key. When the Google Web page is displayed, type Aspen Colorado ski resorts as the search text and then point to the Google Search button.

Step 4
Click the Aspen Snowmass link to display a Web page with a description and links to skiing in Aspen.

Step 3
Click the Google Search button. When the results of the search are displayed, scroll through the links and read the descriptions. Point to the Aspen Snowmass link.

Figure 41   This figure shows how to use a search engine.

shopping, and related subcategories. A subject directory provides categorized lists of links arranged by subject. Using this search tool, you locate a particular topic by clicking links through different levels, moving from the general to the specific.

Computer Viruses and Other Malware

Today, people rely on computers to create, store, and manage critical information. Thus, it is crucial users take measures to protect their computers and data from loss or damage, especially for information that is transmitted over networks. Every unprotected computer is susceptible to a computer virus, worm, Trojan horse, and/or rootkit.

- A computer **virus** is a potentially damaging computer program that affects, or infects, a computer negatively by altering the way the computer works without the user's knowledge or permission. Once the virus infects the computer, it can spread throughout and may damage files and system software, including the operating system.

- A **worm** is a program that copies itself repeatedly, for example in memory or on a network, using up resources and possibly shutting down the computer or network.

- A **Trojan horse** (named after the Greek myth) is a program that hides within or looks like a legitimate program. A certain condition or action usually triggers the Trojan horse. Unlike a virus or worm, a Trojan horse does not replicate itself to other computers.

- A **rootkit** is a program that hides in a computer and allows someone from a remote location to take full control of the computer. Once the rootkit is installed, the rootkit author can execute programs, change settings, monitor activity, and access files on the remote computer.

Computer viruses, worms, Trojan horses, and rootkits are classified as **malware** (short for malicious software), which are programs that act without a user's knowledge and deliberately alter the computer's operations. Users can take several precautions to protect their home and work computers and mobile devices from these malicious infections. For example, users should install an antivirus program and update it frequently. An **antivirus program** protects a computer against viruses by identifying and removing any computer viruses found in memory, on storage media, or on incoming files. Most antivirus programs also protect against other malware. When you purchase a new computer, it often includes antivirus software. The list in Figure 42 summarizes important tips for protecting your computer from viruses and other malware.

Tips for Preventing Viruses and Other Malware

1. Never start a computer with removable media inserted in the drives or plugged in the ports, unless the media are uninfected.

2. Never open an e-mail attachment unless you are expecting it *and* it is from a trusted source.

3. Set the macro security in programs so that you can enable or disable macros. Enable macros only if the document is from a trusted source and you are expecting it.

4. Install an antivirus program on all of your computers. Update the software and the virus signature files regularly.

5. Scan all downloaded programs for viruses and other malware.

6. If the antivirus program flags an e-mail attachment as infected, delete or quarantine the attachment immediately.

7. Before using any removable media, scan the media for malware. Follow this procedure even for shrink-wrapped software from major developers. Some commercial software has been infected and distributed to unsuspecting users.

8. Install a personal firewall program.

9. Stay informed about new virus alerts and virus hoaxes.

Figure 42   With the growing number of new viruses and other malware, it is crucial that users take steps to protect their computers.

Buyer's Guide:
How to Purchase Computers and Mobile Devices

AT SOME POINT, perhaps while you are taking this course, you may decide to buy a computer or mobile device (Figure 43). The decision is an important one and will require an investment of both time and money. Like many buyers, you may have little experience with technology and find yourself unsure of how to proceed. You can start by talking to your friends, coworkers, and instructors about their computers and mobile devices. What type of computers and mobile devices did they buy? Why? For what purposes do they use their computers and mobile devices?

desktop computer

notebook computer

portable media player

smart phone

digital camera

Figure 43 Computers and mobile devices.

How to Purchase a Desktop Computer

A desktop computer sits on or below a desk or table in a stationary location such as a home, office, or dormitory room. Desktop computers are a good option if you work mostly in one place and have plenty of space in a work area. Desktop computers generally provide more performance for your money. Today, manufacturers are placing more emphasis on style by offering bright colors, stylish displays, and theme-based displays so that the computer looks attractive if it is in an area of high visibility. Once you have decided that a desktop computer is most suited to your computing needs, the next step is to determine specific software, hardware, peripheral devices, and services to purchase, as well as where to buy the computer.

① Determine the specific software to use on your computer.

Before deciding to purchase software, be sure it contains the features necessary for the tasks you want to perform. Rely on the computer users in whom you have confidence to help you decide on the software to use. In addition, consider purchasing software that might help you perform tasks at home that you otherwise would perform at another location, such as at school or at work. The minimum requirements of the software you select may determine the operating system (Microsoft Windows, Mac OS, etc.) you need. If you decide to use a particular operating system that does not support software you want to use, you may be able to purchase similar software from other manufacturers.

Many Web sites and trade magazines provide reviews of software products. These Web sites frequently have articles that rate computers and software on cost, performance, and support.

Your hardware requirements depend on the minimum requirements of the software you will run on your computer. Some software requires more memory and disk space than others, as well as additional input, output, and storage devices. For example, suppose you want to run software that can copy one optical disc's contents directly to another optical disc, without first copying the data to the hard disk. To support that, you should consider a desktop computer or a high-end notebook computer, because the computer will need two optical disc drives: one that reads from an optical disc, and one that writes on an optical disc. If you plan to run software that allows your computer to function as an entertainment system, then you will need an optical disc drive, quality speakers, and an upgraded sound card.

② Know the system requirements of the operating system.

After determining the software you want to run on your new computer, the next step is to determine the operating system to use. If, however, you purchase a new computer, chances are it will have the latest version of your preferred operating system (Windows, Mac OS, etc.).

③ Look for bundled software.

When you purchase a computer, it may include bundled software. Some sellers even let you choose which software you want. Remember, however, that bundled software has value only if you would have purchased the software even if it had not been included with the computer. At the very least, you probably will want word processing software and an antivirus program. If you need additional programs, such as a spreadsheet, a database, or presentation software, consider purchasing or downloading Microsoft Office, Microsoft Works, OpenOffice.org, or Sun StarOffice, which include several programs at a reduced price or at no cost.

④ Avoid buying the least powerful computer available.

Once you know the application software you want to use, then consider the following important criteria about the computer's components: (1) processor speed, (2) size and types of memory (RAM) and storage, (3) types of input/output devices, (4) types of ports and adapter cards, and (5) types of communications devices. You also should consider if the computer is upgradeable and to what extent you are able to upgrade. For example, all manufacturers limit the amount of memory you can add. The information in Figure 44 on pages COM 29 and COM 30 can help you determine which computer components are best for you and outlines considerations for specific hardware components. For a sample Base Components worksheet that lists personal computer recommendations for various categories of users, see scsite.com/ic8/buyers.

Considerations for Hardware Components

Card Reader/Writer: A card reader/writer is useful for transferring data directly to and from a memory card, such as the type used in a digital camera, smart phone, or portable media player. Make sure the card reader/writer can read from and write on the memory cards that you use.

Digital Video Capture Device: A digital video (DV) capture device allows you to connect a computer to a video camera or VCR and record, edit, manage, and then write video back on an optical disc or VCR tape. To create quality video (true 30 frames per second, full-sized TV), the digital video capture device should have a USB or FireWire port.

External Hard Disk: An external hard disk can serve many purposes: it can serve as extra storage for your computer, provide a way to store and transport large files or large quantities of files, and provide a convenient way to back up data on other internal and external hard disks. External hard disks can be purchased with the same capacity as any internal disk.

Fingerprint Reader: For added security, you may want to consider purchasing a fingerprint reader. It helps prevent unauthorized access to your computer and also allows you to log onto Web sites quickly via your fingerprint, rather than entering a user name and password each time you access the site. Most use a USB connection and require software installation.

Hard Disk: It is recommended that you buy a computer with at least a 320 GB hard disk if your primary interests are browsing the Web and using e-mail and Microsoft Office suite-type programs; 1 TB if you also want to edit digital photos or if you plan to edit digital video or manipulate large audio files even occasionally; and 2 TB if you will edit digital video, movies, or photos often; store audio files and music; or consider yourself to be a power user. Internal hard disk controllers are available with the RAID option for added data protection.

Joystick/Wheel: If you use the computer to play games, then you will want to purchase a joystick or a wheel. These devices, especially the more expensive ones, provide for realistic game play with force feedback, programmable buttons, and specialized levers and wheels.

Keyboard: The keyboard is one of the more important devices used to communicate with the computer. For this reason, make sure the keyboard you purchase has 101 to 105 keys, is comfortable and easy to use, and has a USB connection. A wireless keyboard should be considered, especially if you have a small desk area.

Microphone: If you plan to record audio or use speech recognition to enter text and commands, then purchase a close-talk headset with gain adjustment support.

Modem: Most computers include a modem so that you can use a telephone line to access the Internet. Some modems also have fax capabilities. Your modem should be rated at 56 Kbps.

Monitor: The monitor is where you will view documents, read e-mail messages, and view pictures. A minimum of a 19" LCD flat-panel monitor is recommended, but if you plan to use the computer for graphic design or game playing, then you may want to purchase a 22" or 27" monitor. Instead of a single large, widescreen monitor, you may want to consider a side-by-side monitor setup.

Mouse: While working with a desktop computer, you use the mouse constantly. Make sure the mouse has a wheel, which acts as a third button in addition to the top two buttons on the left and right. An ergonomic design also is important because your hand is on the mouse most of the time when you are using the computer. A wireless mouse should be considered to eliminate the cord and allow you to work at short distances from the computer.

Optical Disc Drives: Most computers include a DVD±RW combination drive and/or DVD/Blu-ray Disc drive. A DVD±RW or a Blu-ray Disc drive allows you to read optical discs and to write data on (burn) an optical disc. It also will allow you to store and share video files, digital photos, and other large files with other people who have access to a DVD/Blu-ray Disc drive. A Blu-ray Disc has a capacity of at least 25 GB, and a DVD has a capacity of at least 4.7 GB, versus the 650 MB capacity of a CD.

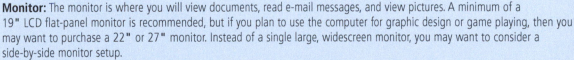

Figure 44 Hardware guidelines. *(continues)*

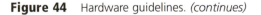

Considerations for Hardware Components

Ports: Depending on how you use the computer, you may need anywhere from 4 to 10 USB ports. USB ports have become the connection of choice in the computer industry. They offer an easy way to connect peripheral devices such as printers, digital cameras, and portable media players. Many computers intended for home or professional audio/video use have built-in FireWire ports. Most personal computers include a minimum of six USB ports, two FireWire ports, and an Ethernet port.

Printer: Your two basic printer choices are ink-jet and laser. Color ink-jet printers cost on average between $50 and $300. Laser printers cost from $200 to $2,000. In general, the less expensive the printer, the lower the resolution and speed, and the more often you are required to change the ink cartridges or toner. Laser printers print faster and with a higher quality than an ink-jet, and their toner on average costs less.

Processor: For a personal computer, an Intel Core i7 processor at 2.93 GHz is more than enough processor power for most home and small office/home office users. Higher-end users, such as large businesses or people who use the computer to play games, should upgrade to faster, more powerful processors.

RAM: RAM plays a vital role in the speed of a computer. Make sure the computer you purchase has at least 2 GB of RAM. If you have extra money to invest in a computer, consider increasing the RAM. The extra money for RAM will be well spent because more RAM typically translates into more speed.

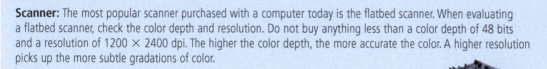

Scanner: The most popular scanner purchased with a computer today is the flatbed scanner. When evaluating a flatbed scanner, check the color depth and resolution. Do not buy anything less than a color depth of 48 bits and a resolution of 1200 × 2400 dpi. The higher the color depth, the more accurate the color. A higher resolution picks up the more subtle gradations of color.

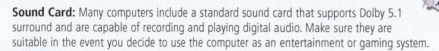

Sound Card: Many computers include a standard sound card that supports Dolby 5.1 surround and are capable of recording and playing digital audio. Make sure they are suitable in the event you decide to use the computer as an entertainment or gaming system.

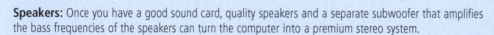

Speakers: Once you have a good sound card, quality speakers and a separate subwoofer that amplifies the bass frequencies of the speakers can turn the computer into a premium stereo system.

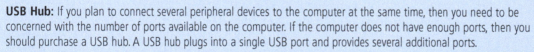

USB Flash Drive: If you work on different computers and need access to the same data and information, then this portable flash memory device is ideal. USB flash drive capacity typically varies from 1 GB to 32 GB.

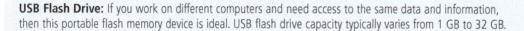

USB Hub: If you plan to connect several peripheral devices to the computer at the same time, then you need to be concerned with the number of ports available on the computer. If the computer does not have enough ports, then you should purchase a USB hub. A USB hub plugs into a single USB port and provides several additional ports.

Video Card: Most standard video cards satisfy the monitor display needs of most home and small office users. If you use your home computer to play games or if you are a graphic designer, you will want to upgrade to a higher quality video card. The higher refresh rates will further enhance the display of games, graphics, and movies.

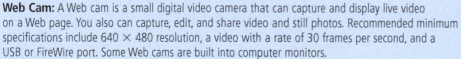

Web Cam: A Web cam is a small digital video camera that can capture and display live video on a Web page. You also can capture, edit, and share video and still photos. Recommended minimum specifications include 640 × 480 resolution, a video with a rate of 30 frames per second, and a USB or FireWire port. Some Web cams are built into computer monitors.

Wireless LAN Access Point: A wireless LAN access point allows you to network several computers, so that multiple users can share files and access the Internet through a single Internet connection. Each device that you connect requires a wireless card or wireless capability. A wireless LAN access point can offer a range of operations up to several hundred feet, so be sure the device has a high-powered antenna.

Figure 44   Hardware guidelines. *(continued)*

Computer technology changes rapidly, meaning a computer that seems powerful enough today may not serve your computing needs in several years. In fact, studies show that many users regret not buying a more powerful computer. To avoid this, plan to buy a computer that will last for at least two to three years. You can help delay obsolescence by purchasing the fastest processor, the most memory, and the largest hard disk you can afford. If you must buy a less powerful computer, be sure you can upgrade it with additional memory, components, and peripheral devices as your computer requirements grow.

5 Consider upgrades to the mouse, keyboard, monitor, printer, microphone, and speakers.

You use these peripheral devices to interact with the computer, so make sure they are up to your standards. Review the peripheral devices listed in Figure 44 and then visit both local computer dealers and large retail stores to test the computers and devices on display. Ask the salesperson which input and output devices would be best for you and whether you should upgrade beyond the standard product. Consider purchasing a wireless keyboard and wireless mouse to eliminate wires on your desktop. A few extra dollars spent on these components when you initially purchase a computer can extend its usefulness by years.

6 Determine whether to use a broadband or dial-up connection to access the Internet.

If your computer has a modem, you can access the Internet using a standard telephone line. Ordinarily, you call a local or toll-free 800 number to connect to an Internet access provider. Using a dial-up Internet connection usually is relatively inexpensive but slow.

Broadband connections (cable, DSL, fiber, radio signals, or satellite) provide much faster Internet connections, which are ideal if you want faster file download speeds for software, digital photos, digital video, and music. As you would expect, they can be more expensive than a dial-up connection. If you want to use a broadband connection, your computer should have an Ethernet card installed, unless you are using a wireless broadband connection such as WiMax or 3G. If you will be using a dial-up connection, your computer should have a modem installed.

7 Use a worksheet to compare computers, services, and other considerations.

You can use a separate sheet of paper to take notes about each vendor's computer and then summarize the information on a worksheet. For a sample worksheet that compares prices for a PC or a Mac, see scsite.com/ic8/buyers. Most companies advertise a price for a base computer that includes components housed in the system unit (processor, RAM, sound card, video card, network card),

hard disks, optical disc drives, a keyboard, mouse, monitor, printer, speakers, and modem. Be aware, however, that some advertisements list prices for computers with only some of these components. Monitors and printers, for example, often are not included in a base computer's price. Depending on how you plan to use the computer, you may want to invest in additional or more powerful components. When comparing the prices of computers, make sure you are comparing identical or similar configurations.

8 If you are buying a new computer, you have several purchasing options: buying from a school bookstore, a local computer dealer, a local large retail store, or ordering by mail via telephone or the Web.

Each purchasing option has certain advantages. Many college bookstores, for example, sign exclusive pricing agreements with computer manufacturers and, thus, can offer student discounts. Local dealers and local large retail stores, however, more easily can provide hands-on support. Mail-order companies that sell computers by telephone or online via the Web (Figure 45) often provide the lowest prices, but extend less personal service. Some major mail-order companies, however, have started to provide next-business-day, on-site services. A credit card usually is required to buy from a mail-order company.

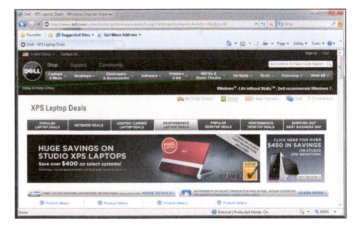

Figure 45 Mail-order companies, such as Dell, sell computers online.

9 If you are buying a used computer, stay with name brands such as Dell, Apple, HP, and Gateway.

Although brand-name equipment can cost more, most brand-name computers have longer, more comprehensive warranties, are better supported, and have more authorized centers for repair services. As with new computers, you can purchase a used computer from local computer dealers, local large retail stores, or mail order via the telephone or the Web. Classified ads and used computer sellers offer additional outlets for purchasing used computers.

10 If you have a computer and are upgrading to a new one, then consider selling or trading in the old one.

If you are a replacement buyer, your older computer still may have value. If you cannot sell the computer through the classified ads, via a Web site, or to a friend, then ask if the computer dealer will buy your old computer.

An increasing number of companies are taking trade-ins, but do not expect too much money for your old computer. Other companies offer to recycle your old computer free or for a fee.

11 Be aware of hidden costs.

Before purchasing, be sure to consider any additional costs associated with buying a computer, such as an additional telephone line, a broadband modem, an uninterruptible power supply (UPS), computer furniture, a USB flash drive, paper, and computer training classes you may want to take. Depending on where you buy the computer, the seller may be willing to include some or all of these in the computer purchase price.

12 Consider more than just price.

The lowest-cost computer may not be the best long-term buy. Consider such intangibles as the vendor's time in business, regard for quality, and reputation for support. If you need to upgrade a computer often, you may want to consider a leasing arrangement, in which you pay monthly lease fees, but can upgrade or add on to your computer as your equipment needs change. No matter what type of buyer you are, insist on a 30-day, no-questions-asked return policy on the computer.

13 Avoid restocking fees.

Some companies charge a restocking fee of 10 to 20 percent as part of their money-back return policy. In some cases, no restocking fee for hardware is applied, but it is applied for software. Ask about the existence and terms of any restocking policies before you buy.

14 Use a credit card to purchase a new computer.

Many credit cards offer purchase protection and extended warranty benefits that cover you in case of loss of or damage to purchased goods. Paying by credit card also gives you time to install and use the computer before you have to pay for it. Finally, if you are dissatisfied with the computer and are unable to reach an agreement with the seller, paying by credit card gives you certain rights regarding withholding payment until the dispute is resolved. Check your credit card terms for specific details.

15 Consider purchasing an extended warranty or service plan.

If you use your computer for business or require fast resolution to major computer problems, consider purchasing an extended warranty or a service plan through a local dealer or third-party company. Most extended warranties cover the repair and replacement of computer components beyond the standard warranty. Most service plans ensure that your technical support calls receive priority response from technicians. You also can purchase an on-site service plan that states that a technician will arrive at your home, work, or school within 24 hours. If your computer includes a warranty and service agreement for a year or less, consider extending the service for two or three years when you buy the computer.

How to Purchase a Notebook Computer

If you need computing capability when you travel or to use in lectures or meetings, you may find a notebook computer to be an appropriate choice. The guidelines mentioned in the previous section also apply to the purchase of a notebook computer. The following are additional considerations unique to notebook computers, including netbooks and Tablet PCs.

1 Determine which computer fits your mobile computing needs.

Before purchasing a notebook computer, you need to determine whether a traditional notebook computer, netbook, or Tablet PC will meet your needs. If you spend most of your time working on spreadsheets, writing and/or editing documents, sending and responding to e-mail messages, or using the Internet, then a traditional notebook computer will suffice. If your primary use will be to access the Internet while traveling and you are not concerned as much with processing power or hard disk capacity, consider a netbook. If you need a computer in class or you spend more time in meetings than in your office, then the Tablet PC may be the answer. Before you invest money in a Tablet PC, however, determine which programs you plan to use on it. You should not buy a Tablet PC simply because it is an interesting type of computer.

2 Purchase a notebook computer with a sufficiently large screen.

Active-matrix screens display high-quality color that is viewable from all angles. Less expensive, passive-matrix screens sometimes are difficult to see in low-light conditions and cannot be viewed from an angle.

Notebook computers typically include a 12.1-inch, 13.3-inch, 14.1-inch, 15.4-inch, or 17-inch display. Netbooks have screens as small as 7 inches. For most users, a 14.1-inch display is satisfactory. If you intend to use the notebook computer as a desktop computer replacement, however, you may opt for a 15.4-inch or 17-inch display. The WSXGA+ standard (1680 × 1050) is popular with 17-inch displays, so if you intend to watch HD movies on the computer, take this into consideration. Some notebook computers with these larger displays weigh more than 10 pounds, however, so if you travel a lot and portability is essential, you might want a lighter computer with a smaller display. The lightest notebook computers, which weigh less than 3 pounds, are equipped with a 12.1-inch display.

Regardless of size, the resolution of the display should be at least 1024 × 768 pixels. To compare the screen size on various notebook computers, including netbooks and Tablet PCs, visit the company Web sites. Tablet PCs use a digitizer below a standard 10.4-inch motion-sensitive LCD display to make the writing experience on the screen feel like writing on paper. To ensure you experience the maximum benefits from the ClearType technology, make sure the LCD display has a resolution of 800 × 600 in landscape mode and a resolution of 600 × 800 in portrait mode.

3 Experiment with different keyboards, pointing devices, and digital pens.

Notebook computer keyboards, especially netbook keyboards, are far less standardized than those for desktop computers. Some notebook computers, for example, have wide wrist rests, while others have none, and keyboard layouts on notebook computers often vary. Notebook computers also use a range of pointing devices, including touchpads, pointing sticks, trackballs, and, in the case of Tablet PCs, digital pens.

Before purchasing a notebook computer, try various types of keyboards and pointing devices to determine which is easiest for you to use. Regardless of the device you select, you also may want to purchase a standard mouse to use when you are working at a desk or other large surface. Figure 46 compares

Mouse and Digital Pen Operations

Mouse	Digital Pen
Point	Point
Click	Tap
Double-click	Double-tap
Right-click	Tap and hold
Click and drag	Drag

Figure 46 Standard point-and-click of a mouse compared with the gestures made with a digital pen.

the standard point-and-click of a mouse with the gestures made with a digital pen. Other gestures with the digital pen replicate some of the commonly used keys on a keyboard.

4 Make sure the notebook computer you purchase has an optical disc drive.

Most mobile computers include an optical disc drive. Although DVD/Blu-ray Disc drives are slightly more expensive, they allow you to play CDs, DVDs, and Blu-ray Discs using your notebook computer and hear the sound through earbuds. If you decide to purchase a netbook, it might not include an optical disc drive. Instead, you might need to purchase an external optical disc drive.

5 If necessary, upgrade the processor, memory, and disk storage at the time of purchase.

As with a desktop computer, upgrading a notebook computer's memory and disk storage usually is less expensive at the time of initial purchase. Some disk storage is custom designed for notebook computer manufacturers, meaning an upgrade might not be available in the future. If you are purchasing a lightweight notebook computer or Tablet PC, then it should include at least an Intel Core 2 Quad processor, 2 GB RAM, and 250 GB of storage. If you are purchasing a netbook, it should have an Intel Atom processor, at least 1 GB RAM, and 120 GB of storage.

6 The availability of built-in ports and slots and a USB hub on a notebook computer is important.

A notebook computer does not have much room to add adapter cards. If you know the purpose for which you plan to use the notebook computer, then you can determine the ports you will need. Netbooks typically have fewer ports than traditional notebook computers and Tablet PCs. Most notebook computers include common ports, such as a video port, audio port, network port, FireWire port, and multiple USB ports. If you plan to connect the notebook computer to a television, however, then you will need a PC to TV port. To optimize television viewing, you may want to consider DisplayPort, DVI, or HDMI ports. If you want to connect to networks at school or in various offices via a network cable, make sure the notebook computer you purchase has a network port. If the notebook computer does not contain a network port, you will have to purchase an external network card that slides into an expansion slot in your computer, as well as a network cable. You also may want to consider adding a card reader.

7 If you plan to use your notebook computer for note-taking at school or in meetings, consider a convertible Tablet PC.

Some computer manufacturers have developed convertible Tablet PCs that allow the screen to rotate 180 degrees on a central hinge and then fold down to cover the keyboard (Figure 47). You then can use a digital pen to enter text or drawings into the computer by writing on the screen. Some notebook computers have wide screens for better viewing and editing, and some even have a screen on top of the unit in addition to the regular screen. If you spend much of your time attending lectures or meetings, then the slate Tablet PC is ideal. With a slate Tablet PC, users can attach a removable keyboard.

Figure 47 A convertible Tablet PC.

8 If you purchase a Tablet PC, determine whether you require multi-touch technology.

Newer operating systems now support hardware with multi-touch technology. If you choose an operating system that supports this technology, the Tablet PC also must support this technology.

9 Purchase a notebook computer with an integrated Web cam.

If you will be using a notebook computer to connect to the Internet and chat with friends online, consider purchasing one with an integrated Web cam.

10 Check with your wireless carrier to see if it offers netbooks for sale.

Most wireless carriers now offer wireless data plans allowing you to connect to the Internet from almost anywhere with a cell phone signal. Some wireless carriers now are selling netbooks with built-in capability to connect wirelessly to the Internet using a wireless data plan.

11 Purchase a notebook computer with a built-in wireless network connection.

A wireless network connection (Bluetooth, Wi-Fi a/b/g/n, WiMAX, etc.) can be useful when you travel or as part of a home network. Increasingly more airports, hotels, schools, and cafés have wireless networks that allow you to connect to the Internet. Many users today are setting up wireless home networks. With a wireless home network, your notebook computer can access the Internet, as well as other computers in the house, from any location to share files and hardware, such as a printer, and browse the Web. Most home wireless networks allow connections from distances of 150 to 800 feet.

12 If you plan to use your notebook computer for long periods without access to an electrical outlet, purchase a second battery.

The trend among notebook computer users today is power and size over battery life. Many notebook computer users today are willing to give up longer battery life for a larger screen, faster processor, and more storage. In addition, some manufacturers typically sell the notebook computer with the lowest capacity battery. For this reason, be careful in choosing a notebook computer if you plan to use it without access to electrical outlets for long periods, such as an airplane flight. You also might want to purchase a second battery as a backup. If you anticipate running the notebook computer on batteries frequently, choose a computer that uses lithium-ion batteries, which last longer than nickel cadmium or nickel hydride batteries.

13 Purchase a well-padded and well-designed carrying case.

An amply padded carrying case will protect your notebook computer from the bumps it will receive while traveling. A well-designed carrying case will have room for accessories such as spare optical discs, pens, and paperwork (Figure 48). Although a netbook may be small enough to fit in a handbag, make sure that the bag has sufficient padding to protect the computer.

Figure 48
A well-designed notebook computer carrying case.

14 If you plan to connect your notebook computer to a video projector, make sure the notebook computer is compatible with the video projector.

You should check, for example, to be sure that your notebook computer will allow you to display an image on the computer screen and projection device at the same time. Also, ensure that the notebook computer has the ports required to connect to the video projector. You also may consider purchasing a notebook computer with a built-in Web cam for video conferencing purposes.

15 For improved security and convenience, consider a fingerprint reader.

More than half a million notebook computers are stolen or lost each year. If you have critical information stored on your notebook computer, consider purchasing one with a fingerprint reader to protect the data if your computer is stolen or lost (Figure 49). Fingerprint security offers a level of protection that extends well beyond the standard password protection. If your notebook computer is stolen, the odds of recovering it improve dramatically with anti-theft tracking software. Manufacturers claim recovery rates of 90 percent or more for notebook computers using their product. For convenience, fingerprint readers also allow you to log onto several Web sites in lieu of entering user name and password information.

Figure 49 Fingerprint reader technology offers greater security than passwords.

16 Review the docking capabilities of the Tablet PC.

The Tablet Technology in the Windows operating system supports a grab-and-go form of docking, so that you can pick up and take a docked Tablet PC with you, just as you would pick up a notepad on your way to a meeting (Figure 50).

Figure 50 A Tablet PC docked to create a desktop computer with the Tablet PC as the monitor.

How to Purchase a Smart Phone

You probably will use a smart phone more often than other mobile devices. For this reason, it is important to choose a phone that is available through your preferred wireless carrier, available in your price range, and offers access to the features you will use most frequently. This section lists guidelines you should consider when purchasing a smart phone.

1 Choose a wireless carrier and plan that satisfies your needs and budget.

Multiple wireless carriers exist today, and each one offers a different line of smart phones. For example, the Samsung Alias is available only through Verizon Wireless. Alternatively, some smart phones, such as the BlackBerry line of smart phones, are available from multiple wireless carriers. Before deciding on a smart phone, you first should research the wireless carriers in your area, and be sure to ascertain whether the coverage is acceptable. Additionally, compare the calling plans for the various carriers and determine which one best meets your needs. Once you have determined the wireless carrier to use, you then can choose from one of their available smart phones. Once you purchase a smart phone, most carriers allow you to perform a risk-free evaluation for 30 days. If you are not satisfied with the phone or its performance, you can return the phone and pay only for the service you have used.

2 Decide on the size, style, and weight of the smart phone that will work best for you.

Smart phones are available in various sizes, weights, shapes, and colors. Some people prefer larger, heavier phones because they feel that they are more durable, while others prefer smaller, lightweight phones for easy portability. Some smart phones are flip phones, meaning that you have to open the phone (like a clamshell) to display the screen and keypad, some open by sliding the phone, and others do not need to be opened to use them. Figure 51 shows various smart phone styles.

Figure 51 Various smart phone styles.

❸ Determine whether you prefer a touch screen, keypad, or mini-keyboard.

Modern smart phones provide various ways to enter text. During the past several years, smart phones with touch screens as their primary input device have been penetrating the market. Some smart phone users prefer touch screens because the phone does not require additional space for a keypad or mini-keyboard, but others find it more difficult to type on a touch screen. Most newer smart phones with touch screens also include handwriting recognition. Smart phones with keypads might make it easier to type for some users, but others do not like the unfamiliar feeling of keys arranged in alphabetical order. In addition, you often have to press the keys multiple times before reaching the letter you want to type. Mini-keyboards are available on some smart phones, such as the BlackBerry and Samsung Alias. Mini-keyboards provide a key for each letter, but the keys are significantly smaller than those on a standard keyboard. Most smart phone users type on mini-keyboards using their thumbs.

❹ If you will be synchronizing your smart phone with a program on your computer, select a smart phone that is compatible with the program you wish to use.

Programs such as Microsoft Outlook allow you to synchronize your e-mail messages, contacts, and calendar with your smart phone. If you would like this functionality, purchase a smart phone that can synchronize with Microsoft Outlook. Similarly, if your company uses a BlackBerry Enterprise server or Microsoft Exchange server, you should consider purchasing a smart phone that can synchronize, either using wires or wirelessly, with those servers.

❺ Compare battery life.

Any smart phone is useful only if it has the power required to run. Talking and using the Internet on your smart phone will shorten battery life more quickly than when the phone is powered on but not in use. If you have a choice, be sure to purchase a battery that will allow the phone to function all day. Pay particular attention to the talk time and standby time. If you plan to talk on the phone more than the advertised talk time, you might consider purchasing a second battery or an extended battery if your phone supports it.

❻ Make sure your smart phone has enough memory and storage.

If you are using the smart phone to send and receive picture, video, and e-mail messages, and to store music, purchase a memory card that not only is compatible with your computer and smart phone, but also has adequate storage space for your messages and files. If you purchase a memory card and eventually fill it, you easily can transfer the data to a larger memory card.

❼ Check out the accessories.

Determine which accessories you want for the smart phone. Accessories include carrying cases, screen protectors, synchronization cradles and cables, and car chargers.

How to Purchase a Portable Media Player

Portable media players are becoming the preferred device for listening to music and watching videos on the go. When choosing a portable media player, it is important to consider features and characteristics other than the physical size and amount of storage space. This section lists guidelines you should consider when purchasing a portable media player.

❶ Choose a device with sufficient storage capacity.

Audio and video files can consume a great deal of storage space, so be sure to purchase a portable media player that has enough capacity to store your audio and video files. You also should consider approximately how many media files you acquire each year, and make sure that your device has enough storage space to accommodate these files for years to come.

❷ Determine which file formats your new portable media player should support and how you will add files to your library.

Some portable media players are designed to accept new audio and video files only through a program installed on a computer. For example, it is easiest to add media files to an iPod using the iTunes program. Other portable media players connect to a computer using a cable and are displayed in Windows as a removable disk. You then can add files to the media player by dragging the files to the removable disk icon in Windows. The portable media player must support the file formats you are using. You can determine the file format by looking at the file extension on the media files you wish to transfer to your portable media player. Before purchasing a portable media player, make sure that it can support the file formats you are using.

❸ Consider a portable media player that can play video.

Some users prefer to watch videos on their portable media player in addition to playing music. You typically can download videos for portable media players less expensively than purchasing the movie on a DVD/Blu-ray Disc. Although the display on a portable media player is small, many still find entertainment value because they are able to watch videos while waiting for a bus, on an airplane, or at other locations where they otherwise might not have anything to occupy them.

❹ Read reviews about the sound quality on the portable media players you are considering.

Sound quality may vary greatly among portable media players. If you are unable to try the portable media player before buying it, read reviews and make sure that those reviewing the devices find the sound quality to be acceptable. You also may consider purchasing higher-quality earbuds or headphones to enhance the sound quality.

❺ Select a size and style that works best for you.

Portable media players are available in various shapes and styles. For example, Apple offers the iPod shuffle, iPod nano, iPod classic, and iPod touch (Figure 52). Each type of iPod varies in size and style, and some have capabilities (such as video) that others do not. Choose a size and style that meets your needs and fits your personality.

Figure 52 Portable media players are available in different shapes, styles, and colors.

❻ Check out additional memory cards.

Most portable media players have internal storage for your media files. If you wish to increase the available storage, consider purchasing a portable media player that allows you to increase storage capacity by inserting memory cards. Similar to most computers, it is less expensive initially to purchase the largest amount of storage that you can afford, but it is helpful to be able to increase your storage at a later date.

❼ Consider rechargeable batteries.

Although most portable media players include rechargeable batteries, some still use traditional alkaline batteries. Portable

media players sometimes can last for only a few hours on alkaline batteries, and battery replacement can be costly. Rechargeable batteries often last longer and create less waste. If you are not near a power source, you are unable to recharge the batteries when they die. With alkaline batteries, you simply can insert new ones and continue enjoying your player.

❽ Stay within your budget.

As previously mentioned, portable media players are available in a variety of shapes and sizes, and they also are available with various storage capacities. When shopping for a portable media player, be realistic when you consider how you will use the device, as well as how much storage you require. Purchasing the latest and greatest device is not always the best option, and the cost can exceed what you care to spend.

How to Purchase a Digital Camera

Both amateur and professional photographers now are mostly purchasing digital cameras to meet their photography needs. Because digital cameras with new and improved features regularly are introduced to the marketplace, consumers should know how to compare the differences among the multiple cameras that are available. This section lists guidelines you should consider when purchasing a digital camera.

❶ Determine the type of digital camera that meets your needs.

Various types of digital cameras exist, including point-and-shoot cameras, field cameras, and studio cameras. Point-and-shoot cameras typically fit in your pocket and meet the needs of most general consumers. Field cameras, which often are used by photojournalists, are portable but flexible. Field cameras allow photographers to change lenses and use other attachments, and also are more customizable than point-and-shoot cameras. Studio cameras are used in photo studios and are stationary. These cameras give you the widest range of lenses and settings.

❷ The digital camera with the highest resolution is not always the best.

Many consumers mistakenly believe that the digital camera with the highest resolution is the best camera for their needs.

A higher resolution increases quality and clarity of your photos, as well as the size at which you can print the photos before noticing degradation in quality. If you never plan to print photos larger than 8" × 10", for example, you do not need a camera with a resolution greater than 5 megapixels. Many cameras available today advertise higher resolutions, but taking pictures at these high resolutions can use valuable storage space. Just because your camera can take a 10-megapixel photo does not mean that you always should set the resolution to 10 megapixels.

❸ Consider size and weight.

Digital cameras are available in various sizes and weights. Some people prefer smaller, lighter cameras because they are easier to transport and take up less space. Others prefer bulkier, heavier cameras because the weight helps steady them to take a clearer picture. Many digital cameras also include an image stabilization feature that reduces the possibility of a blurry picture if you move your hands slightly while taking the picture. Some also believe that heavier cameras are of better quality, although that seldom is true. When choosing a digital camera, practice taking pictures with it and select one that feels comfortable and natural.

❹ Different cameras require different memory cards.

When purchasing a digital camera, pay careful attention to the type of memory card the camera uses. Many use SD cards, some use xD Picture cards, and some use CompactFlash memory cards. Some memory cards are more expensive to replace than others, and some have a higher capacity than other cards. If you take a lot of pictures, purchase a camera that supports a memory card with a higher storage capacity so that you can avoid carrying multiple memory cards. You also might consider purchasing a camera that uses a memory card that is compatible with your other mobile devices.

❺ Photo editing features can save you time.

Some digital cameras have integrated tools that allow you to edit photos directly from the camera. For instance, you may be able to crop photos, change the brightness, or remove red-eye effects. Editing photos directly on the camera after taking them can save you from editing multiple photos at once when you transfer them to a computer. The photo editing capabilities available on digital cameras are limited when compared to photo editing programs, but in many cases they can edit a photo to your satisfaction.

❻ Make sure that you can see the LCD screen easily.

LCD screens on digital cameras allow you to configure the settings, frame a shot before taking it, and preview photos after taking them. LCD screens vary by inches, so select a camera with a screen that does not require you to strain your eyes to view. This is especially important if the camera you are considering does not have a viewfinder, because you then will be required to use the display to frame your shots.

❼ Determine whether your pictures will require you to zoom.

If you plan to take pictures of people or objects that require you to zoom in, select a digital camera that has a high optical zoom. An optical zoom enlarges the subject by adjusting the camera lens, whereas a digital zoom uses formulas built into the camera to magnify images. Optical zooms, as opposed to digital zooms, often result in a higher quality photo. While a digital zoom might be capable of magnifying objects that are 100 feet away, the photo will suffer a loss of quality.

❽ Price is important.

As with all other devices, purchase a digital camera that does not exceed your budget. If you find a great camera that is available for more than you are willing to spend, consider locating a camera with a slightly lower resolution, an alternate brand, or a smaller screen. Digital cameras can last well beyond five years if properly maintained, so consider this a longer-term investment that will create memories lasting you a lifetime.

❾ Know your batteries.

Some digital cameras require replaceable alkaline or rechargeable batteries (often AA or AAA), and others have a rechargeable battery. Similar to batteries in portable media players, using disposable batteries in digital cameras can get expensive, and they may not last as long as rechargeable battery packs. Digital camera battery life is not measured in hours (as is the case with smart phones and portable media players); instead, it is measured in how many pictures can be taken on a single charge or set of batteries. Turning off the LCD screen and flash when you take pictures can help to extend battery life.

❿ Purchase accessories.

Accessories that are available for digital cameras include carrying cases, extra batteries and battery chargers, and extra memory cards (Figure 53). Carrying cases can help protect your digital camera, especially while traveling, and the extra batteries and chargers can stay inside your carrying case so that they are readily available should you need them. Screen protectors can help protect the LCD screen on your digital camera.

Figure 53   Digital camera accessories include memory cards, cases, batteries, and battery chargers.

Learn It Online

Instructions

To complete the Learn It Online exercises, start your browser, click the address bar, and then enter the Web address scsite.com/ic8/learn. When the Introduction to Computers Learn It Online page is displayed, click the link for the exercise you want to complete and then read the instructions.

1 Chapter Reinforcement TF, MC, and SA
A series of true/false, multiple choice, and short answer questions that test your knowledge of the chapter content.

2 Flash Cards
An interactive learning environment where you identify key terms associated with displayed definitions.

3 Practice Test
A series of multiple choice questions that test your knowledge of chapter content and key terms.

4 Who Wants To Be a Computer Genius?
An interactive game that challenges your knowledge of chapter content in the style of a television quiz show.

5 Wheel of Terms
An interactive game that challenges your knowledge of chapter key terms in the style of the television show *Wheel of Fortune*.

6 Crossword Puzzle Challenge
A crossword puzzle that challenges your knowledge of key terms presented in the chapter.

Case Studies

1. Computers are ubiquitous. Watching television, driving a car, using a credit card, ordering fast food, and the more obvious activity of typing a research paper all involve interaction with computers. Make a list of every computer you can recall that you encountered over the past week (be careful not to limit yourself just to the computers you see). Consider how each computer is used. How were the tasks the computers performed done before computers existed? Do you feel computers have a positive impact on people and organizations? Write a brief report and submit it to your instructor.

2. The Internet has had a tremendous impact on organizations. For some organizations, that influence has not been positive. For example, surveys suggest that as a growing number of people make their own travel plans online, travel agents are seeing fewer customers. Use the Web to research organizations that have been affected negatively by the Internet. What effect has the Internet had? How can the organization compete with the Internet? Do you feel that computers might replace humans entirely in the workforce? Why or why not? Write a brief report and submit it to your instructor.

3. As notebook computers become more affordable, an increasing number of college students are purchasing them to use instead of using computers available on campus. As a new college student, you also would like to purchase a notebook computer for your coursework. Shop online for a notebook computer that you believe will be sufficient for your major. Some schools have suggested notebook computer configurations that can assist in your search. Once you find a notebook computer, write a brief report describing the computer (include the brand, model, configuration information, and price), and submit it to your instructor.

4. Today, the functional lines among mobile devices seem blurred. Your cell phone has a digital camera; your portable media player has wireless Internet access; and your game console plays videos and connects to the Internet. These are examples of technological convergence, a process in which separate technologies merge in single products. Write a brief report on how your favorite mobile device is an example of convergence, listing the various technologies that it uses.

Index

Photo Credits